ENCORE SEASONS

Thomas Peter Bennett

Goose River Press
Waldoboro, Maine

Copyright © 2017 Thomas Peter Bennett

All rights reserved. No part of this book may be reproduced in any form without written permission from the publisher, except by a reviewer who may quote brief passages in a review to be printed in a newspaper or magazine.

Library of Congress Card Number: 2017936549

ISBN: 978-1-59713-178-0

First Printing, 2017

Cover design by Charlotte Staub Thomas.
Photographs by Gudrun Dorothea Bennett.

Published by
Goose River Press
3400 Friendship Road
Waldoboro ME 04572
e-mail: gooseriverpress@roadrunner.com
www.gooseriverpress.com

*To everything there is a season,
and a time to every purpose ...*
— Ecclesiastes 3:1

Contents

Acknowledgements//vi

Preface//vii

PRELUDE//ix

AUTUMN//7

WINTER//23

MOCKINGBIRD INTERLUDE//35

SPRING//41

SUMMER//57

About the Author//76

Acknowledgements

The poems in this collection are mostly new and written after November 2015. "Thanksgiving Aerobatics," "Crow Winter," and "Hold Outs" were published in *Goose River Anthology, 2016*; four others benefited from an early 2016 reading at Bookstore1Sarasota in Florida. "Winter Break: In Florida" includes three selected poems from *Goose River Anthology, 2013*: "January Hike," Snowbird," and "Sunny Ice Man." "After the Rain" in the section "Summer" is from *Goose River Anthology, 2015*. "Midnight Call" and "After the Rain," both in the section entitled "Spring," appeared in print earlier with acknowledgements in Aquarius (Longview Press, 1993). The verse that opened this book is Ecclesiastes 3:1, from the St. James version of the *Bible*. The reference "Bloom where you are planted" is a summary of Jeremiah, Chapter 29.

I greatly appreciate the efforts of Deborah J. Benner, editor of the *Anthology* and **Goose River Press** in Waldoboro, Maine, as well as Georgia Court and the staff of **Bookstore1Sarasota**. I also wish to thank my many new Riderwood neighbors who advised me about various aspects of these poems, and offered criticism and encouragement. In addition, I would like to thank Charlotte Staub Thomas for her guidance and cover design and Gudrun Dorothea Bennett for providing photographs and her continuing support for *Encore Seasons*.

Preface

After a decade of retirement—what I dubbed "perpetual sabbaticals"—my wife and I began to consider what to do next, and when. After conversations, data collection and analysis, site visits, and gathering firsthand accounts, we decided to move from our long-time home on Florida's Braden River to an apartment in a large, suburban, college-campus-like retirement community in Maryland. We were attracted by its residents and staff and by what we termed its "encore retirement" services and amenities: close proximity to the homes of our son and daughter, college and university communities, parks and trails, and the cultural comforts of Washington, DC.

However, any move brings challenges. Encore retirement, which involves a major downsizing relocation, has become more common in our mobile society and is a major life transition. Having lived in many places, I adapted to our new home by drawing encouragement from Jeremiah's biblical admonition that I had heard summarized as a child: "Bloom where you are planted." Encore retirement and relocation provide many needs and opportunities to adapt. Accordingly, the poems in this collection began to bloom after we planted ourselves at Riderwood Village near Silver Spring, Maryland.

These poems are about nature, its plants, and its animals, from those on our apartment's balcony to those in the courtyard woods and around campus as the seasons changed. The poems are collected in chronologically ordered sections entitled "Prelude," "Autumn," "Winter," "Spring," and "Summer." "Mockingbird Interlude" is a long poem narrating the natural history of a mockingbird throughout the four seasons. The poems reflect my belief that the arts and sciences inform our experience and appreciation in our unending exploration of nature.

I wrote the poems in the seasons after our November 2015 arrival at Riderwood Village. Drafts of "Changing Seasons" and several other poems were crafted during earlier planning visits. During my nature wandering, observation, and musing, flashes of my Florida experiences interjected themselves, and I have included these in selected poems. I have engaged with and written about nature in Maine in the summer and in Florida year round. However, during the changing seasons in Maryland's alien but enchanting ecosystems, I found myself filled with discoveries and a wish to share my experiences though this collection.

PRELUDE

Changing Seasons

After fifty years of blissful upsizing,
    A decade of equalizing, and minor trimming—
Now, agonizing, wrenching, downsizing,
    Saying goodbye to piano, books, paintings
For our encore retirement move.

The Steinway, a family wedding gift,
    Hoisted through the window of our
Third-floor walkup apartment, for
    Mozart to warm our home.

Audubon, Faulkner, Whitman ...
    Texts, monographs, dictionaries ...
Collections of art, history, nature ...
    Abandoned, stored now in Kindle or in clouds.

Paintings sorted, measured, accessed for
    Future hangings or storage, donated to museums ...
Silver, china, crystal: no family member interest ...
    Photo albums and pictures in boxes tossed after
Scanning, cloud and CD archiving.

Our new apartment awaits us
    Seven hundred miles away,
Near our son's and daughter's homes.
Like our immigrant forebears,
    We face a new world
To bloom where we are planted.

Encore Home

With memories of a sub-tropical foliage view
      Along a widening river with mangrove clusters,
Our Florida Room's vista — in a land of one natural season.

We arrived at our new fourth-floor abode,
      Enchanted by panoramic autumn views —
A polychromatic tree canopy festoons a courtyard
      With leaf colors changing from amber to sepia.

Russet leaves crinkling, aging —
      Reflections on landscape cues, life changes and
Florida's endless season :
      Lush foliage, idyllic rivers and rapture skies.

Getting Acquainted

I wander the retirement campus,
    A naturalist in an alien habitat,
Looking, searching for knowns —
    Ah, there —
A mockingbird perched in a dogwood!
    Swoosh —
The mockingbird streaks, lands nearby,
    A large and unfamiliar oak —
White, pin, red, or other?

I amble over, photograph the bark and several leaves
    To identify and become oak-acquainted
For future saunters of discovery.

Outside In

Nature mentors with woodsy views:
Maples, pines, ash, and oaks,
Where lobed leaves parse breezes,
Where needles droop and twist
And leaf bracts quiver.

Overlooking the balcony's bird feeders,
Overlooking the planters, into the woods —
My study window is an observatory
For eyes and cameras to behold
Nature's ever-changing vignettes.

Nature Experience

From balcony and study vistas,
Observe wildlife residents and visitors —
Trees, shrubs, foliage, flowers, fruit, and seeds,
Birds, squirrels, other creatures —
Their daily lives, activities, and behavior;
Smell nature: rain, flowers, dry leaves;
Listen as wind and animals stir leaves and branches,
Contemplate nature's web and its cycles during
Changing encore seasons.

After the Rain

From my study window, I gaze
As raindrops align, evenly spaced,
On the balcony rail
      And randomly drop
Like life's events.

AUTUMN

Autumn Sightings

From the window,
I glimpse yellow flybys —
    Warblers?
    Orioles?
    Finches?
No, they are —
    Yellow maple leaves
In the autumn wind.

Scouts and Immigrants

Balcony feeder with
Seeds, suet, hanging —
    Day 1.
Curious scout arrives,
Quickly perching, taste testing,
Flutters away into the woods.
    Day 2.
Other scouts approach,
Land and peck,
Take one seed each,
Fly away.
Their IDs confirmed:
White-breasted nuthatch and
Black-capped chickadee.
    Day 3.
Flock of nuthatches then
Several chickadees
Perch in nearby oaks, then
Swoop over and balcony-land;
Nibble seeds and suet,
And surge away.

(continued)

Day 4.
Daily visits begin—
Chickadees, nuthatches,
Relaxed snacks at the feeder;
Jabs at suet, and with
Seeds in their beaks, soar to
Nearby tree branches with proof of
Their scout's discovery, leaving
Evidence for me—
An empty feeder on the balcony.

Biochemist Explains Autumn Colors

"What influences autumn colors?"
    He asked.
"Night's length, weather, and leaf pigments,"
    She replied and added,
"Chlorophyll gives leaves their green color.
Carotenoids create yellow, orange, gold, and tawny hues.
Anthocyanins fashion blends of red, purple, and blue,"
    Concluding,
"Long, dry summers, pre-winter cold snaps give shades of brown."

Eco-Crew

Seeds on the balcony floor,
Dropped from the hanging feeder
By visiting finches, nuthatches,
Black-capped chickadees.

A burst of fly-ins:
Dark-eyed juncos
Pick up seeds, clean the mess.

Footsteps on the Balcony

Six rain-dappled autumn leaves,
Mysteriously arrayed two by two,
Mark the autumn spirit's path indoors.
Footprints,
Started at the railing,
End at the door
As chilling winds ruffle nearby trees.

Frosty Morning

Naked trees
Reveal roofs
Glittering with ice crystals.

As the sun's rays glide
Over the shadowed slates,
The ice melts like a glacier in retreat,
Becoming sky-mirrored puddles.

Thanksgiving Acrobatics

A silhouette against the November sky
On a tall oak's highest bare branches; then
A ten-foot leap
      Down, down
Onto a craggy limb in a nearby oak.
A short, lateral jump to a maple's twigs; then
A fast dive
      Twenty feet
To snag a low-hanging bough; then
A floating hop
      To acorn-laden leaves
For a squirrel's feast.

Maple Leaf Message

Glistening and golden
In late autumn's morning light,
Fluttering and clinging
To frosted maple branches,
Defying their winter fate.

I glance through the window
At the freezing, bright leaves,
Tighten my hood,
Adjust my boots,
Brace myself—
I'm not in Florida—
As I leave to hike on.

Hold Outs

As the days shorten,
Three crinkled dry leaves
Cling to a knotty branch
On the naked maple.
They quiver, glistening golden
In late autumn's light,
Challenging winter's lot:
Leaf drop and eco-recycle.

Almost Ready

Maples and poplars are minimalist sculptures
Stripped bare to their limbs and trunks.
Ash foliage is rococo rose-speckled light green,
Nature's new exhibition,
Almost ready for winter's opening.

Autumn's Exit

Tawny leaves,
Like migrating monarchs,
Swarm in the autumn winds.
In the morning sunlight,
Barren branches beam,
Golden brown leaves litter the ground.
Nature arrays the woods for winter.

Winter Preparation

    Sky darkens, temperature plummets—
Bursts of wind-created vortices:
    Brown, rust, and yellow leaves.
Gusts become gales;
    Maples are stripped bare.
Squirrels scamper
    Making nest repairs.

Hanging feeders spill
    Swirling seed squalls.
I cover pansies in their planters,
    Refill feeders, hang suet:
Ready my balcony nest
    For the coming winter.

Evergreens Revealed

In early December, from a chilly balcony,
Through bare branches of oaks and maples,
I see young evergreens.
Invisible during early autumn,
They now soar
Like islands above seas of leaves,
Dark green foliage well adapted
For winter's coming wind, snow, and ice.

WINTER

Snow Flurries

Coming at noon,
Just as predicted;
Stark tree branches
Silently await winter's dusting.

Finches, juncos, and sparrows
Seek tangled twigs for shelter.
Squirrels scurry to bough crannies
For nests and the warmth of dead leaves.

Rapt nuthatches poke-nibble
At balcony suet, serene in snowflakes
As I enjoy the silent overture
Of nature's winter opera.

Crows Transformed

Snowflakes twirling—
    Two crows side by side,
Ebony beaks touching often,
    And one's raised wing
Shelters the other.
    As snowfall continues,
They become snowbirds.

Foggy

On a December morning,
A dark shape landed on a pin oak's high limb.
A hawk?

Its head rotated,
Its rigid tail line straightened,
Its broad tip, a red blur or a sun glint?
Pale breast feathers, orange-tinged?
Streaked or a shadow?
A red-tailed hawk, I guessed.

The fog closed in.
I was left with many doubts;
The bird, a shadowy memory.

Medical Seasons

"It's bloody-nose season,"
    The ER doctor said.
"Get a humidifier for each room;
    Adjust to 40–60 RH."
And weeks later,
    I was told,
"It's arthritis season;
    The cold front moved through,
The pressure and temperature, going down—
    Take Tylenol, rest, bandage the foot,
Stay warm."
    "Interesting," I said.
"Perhaps it's time for you to prescribe
    A Florida winter-break season?"

Winter Break: Florida

1. Hike

    AccuWeather declares:
Very windy, snow,
    If you were there.
Sunshine breezy and humid
    Since you are here.
With memory of Maryland and
    A salubrious breeze at your back,
Hike on in Florida.

2. Snowbird

    I didn't recognize you
In unfamiliar plumage
    As you swam near the dock
Until your body arched,
    And in a graceful dive,
You sliced the water and
    Abruptly bobbed to the surface.
Welcome neighbor, loon!
    Like you, I wear Florida garb
And enjoy the warm waters
    With fish for every meal.

(continued)

3.   Sunny Snowman

    A hard freeze last night
Left powdered ice on the dock.
    Under an azure morning sky,
We scraped and molded
    Shavings of ice to form a
Miniature snowman.
    He had fiddler crab arms,
Sand grains for eyes, and
    A mangrove seed for a nose;
His hat, a jaunty oyster shell.

Crow Winter: Maryland

Rocked by the winter wind,
The maple stands bare
Except for three preening
Ebony crows
Gripping nude branches.

Snowzilla Begins

1:30 p.m.
Snow crystal breezes,
Nuthatches nipping seeds,
Woodpecker drumming suet;
Snowflakes growing, swirling, sticking.

3:30 p.m.
Snow accumulates on balcony railing,
Covers feeder roof, where several
Nuthatches continue feeding;
Juncos retrieve dropped seeds.

6:30 p.m.
Thundersnow and lightning.
Birds, birds, more birds feeding;
Seed husks and suet scraps speckle growing snow heaps.
I leave to stock up on groceries and bird seed.

Mockingbird Enigma

"I can't believe it!" she exclaimed,
Gazing from the study window
On the day after Snowzilla.
"A mockingbird!"

A Florida mirage?
A lost Maryland resident?
A wayward migrant?
A Snowzilla traveler?

The mockingbird flitted
From a snow-covered chair on the balcony
To a side table with evergreen branches
And landed gracefully on the ice.

"I still can't believe it!" she declared,
As the mockingbird turned quickly
And sailed to the nearby feeder,
Then, with a seed in its beak, flew away.

MOCKINGBIRD INTERLUDE

1.
An encore move from Florida to Maryland,
A welcoming mockingbird song
Heard from our balcony,
The glint of the sun on the singer's eye.

2.
On many autumn and winter days,
You've visited outside my study window.
You preen, wind-blown,
And dart from distant to close up
In a holly tree jeweled with ruby fruit.

Did you follow me from Florida?
Now, in our Maryland courtyard,
A solitary mockingbird songster.
Here, grooming yourself;
Your solitary observer watching.

3.
Festivals of winter arrive.
Dazzle me with wing bling,
Jerk-jerk unbolt your wings;
Flaunt the white fan patch on each,
Quickly cloaked again in gray feathers;
Parade and repeat your white flashes;
Expand your tail feathers;
Flash white semaphores of feasting celebration.

(continued)

4.
A January flight of roving mockers
Invade and forage in grasses and bushes
Near the holly tree,
Ready for a raid on remaining berries.

You circle them in a border dance,
Wing flashing and tail fanning,
Screaming a territorial warning:
Loud, repeated churrs, scratchy chat calls.
You alone, five attackers ...

Aroused mockingbird neighbors,
Protecting shared holly berry tree,
Band together and charge the intruders
With dive-bombing tactics, attack rolls, and strident calls —
    Chew, Chewk!
Ch'ch'ch'chick, Chew! Chewk! Chew! —
Send the raiders into ragged retreat.

5.
In early-morning March frost,
Your beak punctures the wind.
Your body size has tripled;
The cold wind inflates
Your hidden overcoat
And powder-puffed feathers.
Your wings become a sheltering cape.
I shiver, watching, thinking
Spring is on the way.

(continued)

6.
Your continuous, restless lusting song
From the depths of the holly tree,
Sporadic through the April day,
Becomes louder, more frequent:
Whistles, trills, airs; day into night.

A male invader mockingbird,
Prowling for a mate,
Flutters, silently watchful
From a neighboring magnolia.

From the holly tree comes
Your laser-focused warning—
Your harsh, dry *chew-chewk* call—
And with a nodding glance,
The lone mocker moves on, and
Your love song begins again.

7.
In May, you sing
A longing tenor aria
From the holly tree.

A passing female pauses
On a nearby dogwood tree.

(continued)

In a flash,
You dive ten feet,
Circle loop,
Back to your perch.
White wings flashing,
Return to your song of love.

8.
Later in May,
He or she?
Twig in beak, prying in holly leaves,
Creeping along a branch toward the trunk.
The start of a nest?

9.
Two in the holly tree, in your
Nest with three blue-green eggs spotted brown.
Every day, you forage, feed, guard;
Your mate alert, bright-eyed,
With feather-quilted eggs.

SPRING

Spring Cleaning

White blossoms fleck tips
    Of cherry branches.
A foraging squirrel,
    Biting a flowering twig,
Scampers up the tree trunk,
    Inserts the spring treasure
Into a nest of sticks and dry leaves,
    Causing winter collectibles—
Bits of twigs, snake skin, and lichens—
    To fly in the late March winds,
Spring-cleaning the nest.

Green Debut

Winter passed with shades of black —
Leaden skies, taupe and onyx tree trunks and branches,
Interspersed with shades of white —
Ivory flakes, creamy swirls, and beige snow crusts.

Now, the trees are shades of green —
Emerald, celadon, harlequin, and chartreuse,
Patchwork foliage with bark stitches,
A subtle spring Monet.

Snake in a Tree?

A gauzy, molted snake skin
    Draped around a bare oak branch,
Pinned to a squirrel's nest,
    Fluttered in the wind.

I watched and wondered —
    Did a snake climb the oak,
Wrap and rub around the limbs,
    Sluff off its aged skin?
Did squirrels attach it to their nest
    As an ominous flag for intruders?
Hypotheses, but what proof?
    Do snakes climb trees?

Young John James Audubon answered,
    "Yes, snakes climb trees,"
In what became a scientific controversy.

Audubon painted a portrait of mockingbirds
    Defending their tree nest against a rattlesnake.
Naturalist George Ord called it artistic imagination:
    "Snakes do not climb trees!"
Audubon published, described more evidence,
    "… snakes ascend to their nests …
    suck the eggs or swallow the young …"

(continued)

Ord said,
"Nonsense, a woodsman's tale."
But ...
    Audubon's field findings were confirmed by others:
    "Snakes do climb trees."
Even so, what of the fluttering snake skin —
    From a snake in the tree?
Or retrieved by squirrels on the ground for
    Their nest in the oak?

Early Spring Invasion

A blackish scout,
Small, chunky, purplish-green iridescent,
Lands and glances nervously around,
Sees no rivals or threats;
Taste-tests suet, samples seeds,
Swiftly flies away.

Minutes later,
Two companions arrive:
Long pointed yellow bills,
Pink legs, and short tails.

Field guide — need a field guide
To identify this Brewer's or rusty blackbird,
Grackle, cowbird, purple martin — or whatever it may be.
I might have seen it in Florida: an invasive nuisance?

Suddenly, flurries of wings swoop:
A constellation, a chattering vulgarity
Of pecking, probing yellow bills
With dazzling ebony bodies on pink stilts.
Flocks of a hundred lookalikes seen on a Florida golf course!
No field guide needed: European starling, Sturnus vulgaris.

The Promise

Pale, mint-green foliage
    With tree bark accents
Flutters as it canopies the courtyard
    Against a cerulean sky,
Veiled in the humid promise
    Of spring showers.

Daffodil green sprouts fill balcony planters,
    Soon with colors, shades, and hues.
Robins, orioles, and hummingbirds
    Will shortly return following
Geese flying in V-formation, now overhead.

Daybreak

Foggy morning —
    An owl hoots.
Dawn mist outlines
    Spider web nests.
A dew drop slithers
    Down a leaf's curve.
Sunrise brightens
    Subtle silver pastel
Treetop boughs.

Morning Changes

Ashen skies at seven
      Darkened at eight.
Rain gently fell.

By nine, a bright spray of light
      Through cirrus-blue skies
Glittered the greening trees.

At ten, a sky of charcoal,
      Snow flurries, and soft, white fluff
Decorated the leaf buds.

At eleven, cotton-ball clouds
      Floated, drifted, expanded, contracted,
Backlit by streaming celestial beams.

Traps

Fog at dawn reveals
    Spiders' web craft.

A dewy sheetweb
    Links grass blades
        And girds weed stalks.

Tension-web filaments
    Tether tree branches.

Filmy domes disperse
    Reflected light from
        Sticky capturing webs.

Attending each web,
    A spider eagerly awaits
        An insect snack.

A Warbler

Plucked a worm from
The dew-dropped grass.

    The warbler—
One of fifty-four species
In seventeen genera
Of Western Hemisphere birds
Peterson called: "Butterflies of ornithology"
    —was unknown to me.

As a peeping birder,
I watched the warbler beating the
Ground with the worm and then
Eating it in one swallow.

Wildflowers

I planted a Middle-Atlantic seed mix
To observe the sprouting,
Growth, and blooming of wildflowers
Unknown to me, a Floridian.

Germs for a cutting garden summer,
Autumn, and winter seed harvest:
To be reborn and bloom here again,
After our move from Florida.

Noah, Where Is Your Ark?

Rain came in late April
Each day, for days ...
"The longest continuous number of days,"
*The Washington Pos*t reported, "Since 1998!"
Several days later, the *Post* heralded: "1947."
Then: "1935," "1899," "1871," and still counting.

Lichen Alfresco

After the rainstorm,
The balcony was garnished
With twigs and branches,
Seasoned with yellow, gray,
And leathery splotches of
Primeval plant life—a
Picnic snack for beetles and slugs.

After the Rain

Is a wonderful
Time for mating
As every chartreuse
Tree frog knows.

SUMMER

Foliage Changes

After autumn's chromatic gamut,
Winter's absolutes and dormancy,
And spring's sunshine foliate tints,
Now, heavy-breathing, transpiring plants.
Summer's swelling leafiness:
Shades of green, an emerald spectrum,
An excited chlorophyll festival.

Awaking

A verdant treescape,
    Dark, somber, motionless,
Awaits a photographer
    To capture its awakening
As light tints add texture and depth
    To rousing foliage at sunrise.

Unseen Acrobat

A burst of shaking leaves
    Startles my balcony reverie;
Down the tree, seconds later,
    Oak leaves crash.
Foliage quakes, ten feet down;
    Then, on the vine-covered ground,
A swishing path of quivering leaves
    Blazed by an unseen acrobat.

Flowers Hardly Noticed

Blue blaze morning glories,
    Blooms throated creamy white
Festoon the balcony rail.

Multicolored petunias,
    A spectrum of alluring flowers
Cascade nearby.

Scarlet and ivory fuchsias,
    Drooping unveiled florets,
Cavort in the breeze.

Hummingbirds and bees
    Invade, race, compete for
Yellow nectar ports on red plastic flowers.

After the Rain

Late afternoon—
    It is copper and green
Outdoors.

Tree trunks and atmosphere
    Are copper;
All else is green—
    Leaves, grass, ferns.
The scene is quiet,
    Still,
Just the rain smell
    And sound of distant thunder.

Ecolights

Miniature twinkles, flickers,
Random bursts at dusk
Among oaks, maples, and poplars.

Firefly luciferase,
Catalyst for luciferin,
Illumines the woods.

Midnight Call

Barred owl calls,
Hoohoo-hoohoo,
Hoohoo-hoohooaw.

I echo eight hoots.

Moonbeams
Glint the trees.
Barred owl calls
Eight hoots, and
The woods darken.

Orientation

A white-breasted nuthatch
Winged from a nearby tree,
Landed upside down on
The balcony wall—
Drop-floated to a hanging
Seed bar and pecked away,
Craftily reaching hidden seeds,
When bottom's up.

To Lure a Mockingbird

"Raisins will do the trick!"
    A Maryland birder explained.

I tried and tried —
Loose raisins on the balcony railing,
Raisins in the hanging feeder, on the floor.
Starlings arrived, feasted,
Then a vulgarity of starlings descended.

Mockingbirds were everywhere in Florida,
Deck, porch, jasmine vines, lawn,
Challenging their image in car mirrors,
The mailbox, displaying their flags of alert —
No temptations were needed.

Forget the past; ask another local birder!

Stormy Evening Ballet

Lightning and thunder
    Transformed the woods
From a darkened stage
    With hidden figures
To a ballet of nature.

Wind and rain choreographed
    Nature's dancing corps.
Maples, ash, oaks, and pines,
    In ageless agile movements,
Tilted, rocked backward,
    Turned, rose, and outstretched
In a thunderous allegro.

Celebrity Tour

Endless chatter, buzz, and speculation
Among media pundits becomes frenzied:
    "Tropical storm or hurricane?"

Celebrity Hermine casually lingers
In a Gulf dressing room for her Florida debut,
    Pondering, "To be or not to be?"
Following only the stage cues
Of Gulf Stream waters and skies above.

The tour continues with guesses and tweets:
    "Threat to the Northeast Coast?"
Hermine … "so close, yet so far."

In an off-shore Atlantic lounge,
As odds change hourly in casino press rooms,
    Betting, "Coastal debut or no?"
The winner is known only
To Atlantic Ocean waters and darkening skies.

Try Oranges for Orioles

I started with orange halves
      Along the balcony railing.
Watching from my study.

Blowflies visited the softening halves,
      A week-long orange vigil.
No orioles!

"Orioles love the color orange!"
      I was told.
Then a bright orange feeder,
      Holders for orange halves, but
No orioles!

"The season's not right,"
      A birder said,
"Eat the oranges!"

Forever Summer

As we sweat toward summer's end,
A season of record highs.
Sunshine, sunshine: hot, very hot, and then
      Ghastly hot.

Balcony plants wilt in early morning.
Water barrel runs dry.
Panting birds sip and splash
In kitchen-refilled water baths.

Where have the cooling rains gone?
Nature's high-pressure system is in control —
A lingering, scorching summer.

Understanding

Our summer lingered:
Record heat and no rain —
While TV-reported rain stormed daily with
Midwestern floods, mayhem, and tragedy.
Our dogwood's leaves changed to a somber color,
Mourning, and umber oak leaves fell.

Transition

The morning glory leaves, lacing
The balcony's railing, are browning;
Several blooms are wilted blue.
Glittering hummingbirds and other visitors,
Their bio-alarms sounding, have flown south.
I gaze beyond, into still woods of amber foliage.

Encore Cycle

An autumn tree canopy,
    Crinkled leaves tinkling
Like bells: memory bells,
    Future bells, as our next
Encore season begins.

About the Author

Thomas Peter Bennett is Florida born. He graduated from Florida State University, earned his PhD in biochemistry from Rockefeller University, and became an assistant professor at Harvard. After a brief tenure as professor at the University of Kentucky, he returned to Florida State University as professor and chair of biological sciences and later served as special assistant to the president. He began his museum work in 1976 as president of the Academy of Natural Sciences of Philadelphia and, after a decade, returned to Florida. At the University of Florida, he was professor and director of the Florida Museum of Natural History for another decade. Continuing as a courtesy professor at the University, Bennett became president of Science Service and the publisher of Science News in Washington, DC. He became executive director of the South Florida Museum in 1998 and emeritus director in 2006. He is the author of many scientific and education articles and books, as well as poems and poetry collections.

His poems have been published in *Poet Talk, Poet, Perspectives in Biology and Medicine, Goose River Anthology, Café Review,* and *Puckerbrush,* among others. His collections include *A Celebration of John and William Bartram, Nature as One Sees It, The River Widens, Hike On,* and others.

Bennett resides with his wife Gudrun Dorothea in Maryland, where he writes and pursues nature, his museum interests, often returning to Florida.